❖ Why Animals Behave the Way They Do

❖ *Eugene J. Walter, Jr.*

Why Animals Behave the Way They Do

ILLUSTRATED WITH PHOTOGRAPHS

Charles Scribner's Sons ❖ *New York*

To my father, who never suspected
what he was getting both of us into
when he started taking me to the zoo.

Photographs courtesy of New York Zoological Society.

Library of Congress Cataloging in Publication Data
Walter, Eugene J.
   Why animals behave the way they do.
   Includes index.
   1.   Animals, Habits and behavior of.
I.   Title.
QL751.W258   591.51   81–4572
ISBN 0–684–16879–0   AACR2

1 3 5 7 9 11 13 15 17 19 QD/C 20 18 16 14 12 10 8 6 4 2
Printed in the United States of America

❖ *Acknowledgments*

About seven and a half years ago I campaigned for and won a new job. The first person I called to share my good news with was my father in St. Louis. "Do you remember what I always wanted to do when I was a kid?" I asked him.

"Sure," he replied, "you always wanted to work in the zoo."

"Well, I finally made it!"

Specifically, I had been hired as Curator of Publications of the New York Zoological Society and Editor of its magazine, *Animal Kingdom*, and I was taking up residence in an office at the Society's flagship operaation, the Bronx Zoo. Through this position I naturally became involved in the Society's wildlife conservation program, a highly respected, international effort that, among its many accomplishments, has been responsible for some remarkable studies of animal behavior and ecology.

For me it has been a rewarding professional and intellectual association; without it I could not have written this book. A book perhaps, but a less substantial, less accurate one. I am much in the debt of William Conway, the Society's General Director; George Schaller, our Director of Conservation; and all the scientific staff at the Zoo for sharing their knowledge with me and for, now and then, setting straight some cockeyed notions about animals. I am particularly grateful to James Doherty, General Curator and Curator of Mammalogy, and Joseph Bell, Scientific Assistant to the Director and Honorary Curator of Ornithology. Two of the most gifted animal people in the world of zoological parks, Jim and Joe reviewed my prose—and corrected it when necessary—steered me to sources that might have taken me months to locate, and made suggestions.

For assistance in the pictorial aspects of this book, I owe much to Bill Meng, Assistant Curator for Photographic Services, who aided me in my search through the Society's collection of some 50,000 negatives. Bill and his associate, Dennis DeMello, were responsible for a high percentage of the fine photos that adorn these pages.

Since portions of this book first appeared as an article in *International Wildlife* magazine, I am thankful to the editors of that publication. Thanks also to friend and fellow author Edward Ricciuti for pointing me in their direction. I would be remiss if I did not also acknowledge the support and kindness of my editor, Lee Deadrick of Charles Scribner's Sons, who first contacted me about this project, then had to exercise considerable patience while I completed it.

❖ Contents

❖ *Introduction*

When did animals begin to behave? Four chimpanzees were riding a motorcycle. Ranging in size from very little—perched nervously up front in the V of the handlebars—to very large, they all wore brightly colored outfits. Short-sleeved pullovers and short pants, much like children's playsuits.

Although the motorized quartet did not travel at reckless speed, their vehicle veered uncomfortably close to other chimps relaxing on chairs along the rear of the stage. A chorus of angry shrieks warned the driver and his crew to keep their eyes on the road. Which they did, next time touring the oval stage without incident.

It was late in the 1930s and "Motorcycle Madness" was but one of the "tricks" that comprised the St. Louis Zoo's chimp show, a fast-paced vaudeville that was the envy of the Brothers Ringling. During the roughly thirty-minute routine, the chimpanzees also rollerskated, performed on trapezes and tight wires, rode elegant, long-tailed ponies and amazingly calm Great Danes, formed a musical combo (demonstrating a distinct preference for rhythm over melody), and entertained a standing-room-only crowd with a dazzling array of acrobatics and amusing antics.

As a youngster growing up in St. Louis, I visited the zoo as often as my father would take me. The clowning chimps were always high on my "must see" list.

As we sat on the arena's bleachers, shielding ourselves from the summer sun as best we could, most of us in the audience probably were dimly aware that, back in the African jungle or wherever it was they came from, chimpanzees did not rollerskate or drive motorcycles or

1

wear costumes. I feel fairly confident in stating that virtually no one in the audience thought about it at all. If we speculated about anything it was probably to marvel at the skill of the human trainer who could teach these not-quite-human creatures to do such things.

On the other hand, what was natural? What *did* they do in the African jungle? For the few who wondered there was precious little information. But a great deal of *mis*information.

Another thirty years passed before a young Englishwoman emerged from those African jungles and began publishing books that related facts, instead of fantasies, about these animals. The reality of chimpanzee behavior can enthrall the observer as much as motorcycling. Possibly more. While chimpanzees still perform at the St. Louis Zoo—albeit in a somewhat more subdued presentation that also stresses the animals' native intelligence and the innate abilities that make it possible for them to perform—the general public has also embraced books and television films offering the "true story" of wildlife with great enthusiasm.

Dr. Jane Goodall, the lady who made the chimps at Tanzania's Gombe Stream famous and brought us fresh insights into their society, is part of a modest scientific explosion. Shortly after World War II zoologists began trekking to the world's rain forests, deserts, polar regions, and grasslands and, using modern scientific techniques and instruments, they began to assemble detailed portraits of wild animals. These field biologists are among the more visible trademarks of the rather new science called ethology, a title derived from the Greek word *ethos*, meaning character.

Ethology aims to investigate and understand animal behavior. Viewed at its simplest level, behavior means doing something—an act, a movement. It may also appear to be doing nothing. Sleep, after all, is behavior.

While observable actions make up the heart of the ethologist's concern, things go on inside the animal that cannot be seen. Thought processes, for example. Plus various chemical reactions. Internal actions often trigger behavior; at other moments they are a response to external goings-on.

Experiments conducted in 1980 at the University of Texas in Houston showed that monkeys score relatively high on tests of memory. Only slightly lower than humans taking the same exams. Remembering is a form of behavior, one that influences more obvious forms.

Certainly an animal's behavior is linked intimately to its anatomical apparatus. A species cannot deviate from its standard method of performing any given function if it lacks the equipment to do so. Cheetahs do not possess the strength to overwhelm their prey as lions do. When a cheetah hunts, it relies mostly on its blazing speed. An exceptionally supple spine snaps in and out, propelling this cat's long legs forward at a rate that sends it flying across the plains.

If you want to survive you must behave. Nearly all animal behavior is a product of what might be called survival strategy, the purpose of which is to maintain life in any environment and to reproduce, continuing life through future generations. That is why each animal species does what it does in its own special way. It works.

Through the long process of evolution some animal species developed the "right" combination of physical and behavioral traits to cope successfully with the demands of their environment. Others, deficient in some way, could not compete and fell by the wayside. Indeed, some animals existed for thousands of years but ultimately lacked the flexibility to adapt to changing conditions. They survive now only as fossils. The ever-popular saber-toothed cats lived on earth far longer than today's lions and tigers have. Yet the saber-tooths fizzled out about 10,000 years ago. Those powerful, but somewhat slow-moving cats, subsisted largely on big, plant-eating animals. Those lumbering behemoths eventually were superceded by smaller, swifter herbivores that could compete more effectively for the available food. As the saber-tooths' prey fell by the wayside of evolutionary progress, so did the big cats.

In effect, nature "programs" behavior into the survivors, coding their genes so that the hereditary combinations necessary for success pass to the next generation and the next and the next. Hence animals are born with knowledge of how to perform in certain circumstances—instant comprehension. We usually call it instinct.

Recently hatched herring gulls know immediately to peck at a red spot on their parents' bills, signaling them—for they are likewise programmed—to regurgitate food so the chicks may satisfy their hunger. No one teaches the baby bird to do that. It just knows.

Yet instinct is not everything. A great many of the survival skills that constitute behavior are acquired as the animal matures. The cheetah mother does not simply wean her cubs and send them off to hunt their own food. She holds classes. The cubs begin by imitating their mother's stalking behavior—the prelude to the chase that gives the hunter an advantage. When the youngsters are more mature, the mother may hunt and capture her prey—for example, a gazelle fawn. Instead of killing it she brings it to her cubs waiting on the sidelines and releases it. If they do not respond, or if their efforts to pursue are inept, Mom will recapture the fawn and again let it go. Soon instinct meshes with learning and the cubs succeed.

Successful learning may not occur on the first trial; the hunting mother may have to repeat the lesson several days running before the trainees fend for themselves. Even then their success rate will be low. It requires drill.

Stating that nearly all animal behavior occurs for the sake of survival is simply a necessary qualification. Quite possibly all behavior is linked to survival but we do not yet have sufficient evidence to make such a sweeping pronouncement. Take the observations reported in 1980 at the University of Wisconsin primate center which indicated that, during the course of mating, female monkeys experience orgasm. Surprising, because orgasms were thought to be a human exclusive. Moreover, the investigators believe that they will uncover evidence of the same sexual response in most other mammals.

The automatic question to an ethologist is: Why? A female need not experience orgasm to produce a baby. Why then does it exist? Mother Nature rarely arranges circumstances just for fun. Does orgasm have survival value? Could be. It's an idea that demands a lot of further study.

These examples barely suggest the infinite variety of animal behavior, which, when viewed against the multiplicity of species, makes the task of the ethologist appear somewhat staggering. Although a new species pops up every now and then, zoologists have thus far identified some 6,000 mammals, 9,200 birds, 6,500 reptiles, 2,500 amphibians, and 32,000 kinds of fish. And these are just the vertebrates! The numbers of invertebrates run into the millions. Insects alone total more than a million.

Considering the obstacles it is surprising that we know as much as we do. Indeed, there are many times more questions than answers at present. Ethologists are like explorers who have barely mapped the first mile in exploring a vast wilderness.

Human behavior muddies the animal behavior picture. People were attempting to comprehend other animals' behavior long before they were able to write about it. Prehistoric folk saw the animals as a source of food or as competitors for food. Understanding animals became vital. Some of the hunters recorded their observations by painting them on the walls of caves. Others fashioned animal figures of clay, stone, or bone. The detail in much of this ancient art indicates that primitive man possessed a fair amount of informal knowledge of the ways of his fellow creatures.

Not until the fourth century B.C. did a more or less scholarly approach to animal behavior appear in western civilization—in the person of Aristotle. The Greek philosopher recorded much about the social structure of honeybee hives, noting the different functions of rulers, workers, and drones. He described the habits of a variety of species—courtship displays, mating behavior, for example—and he related physical structure to function.

Although many of his observations remain sound today, the great Greek thinker sometimes went astray. Noting the disappearance of many birds during cold weather, Aristotle concluded that the birds wintered beneath the sea. Despite that fluff he was on the right track toward the concept of migration since he also noted alterations in avian physiology that coincided with climatic seasonal changes.

Perhaps Aristotle's greatest contribution was his recognition of what eventually came to be called instinct: powerful innate drives that caused all members of any given species to respond in an identical manner within a similar set of circumstances.

The Aristotelian notions were soon overshadowed by views espoused by the disciples of another Greek of some repute: Plato. The Platonic crowd had a neat way of conjuring up principles, then tracking down proof to substantiate the principles. Contradictions were ignored if they couldn't be reshaped to the contours of the all-important principle. Within such a philosophical straitjacket animals were regarded as sort of substandard humans.

The viewpoint was cockeyed enough; worse, it caught on. Especially during the medieval era in Europe with Christianity on the ascendance and cathedrals rising along with lofty aspirations. Hewing to the Platonic line, early Christian theologians did not observe animals so much as tuck them into a philosophical scheme, explaining behavior according to plan and thereby avoiding sticky arguments.

Even though Aristotle's writings about the animal world influenced learned clergymen and scholastics such as St. Thomas Aquinas, as well as Jewish and Islamic intellectuals of the period, the Platonic views were embraced by church and congregation alike. Man, the supreme earthly being, held dominion over all other creatures. Animals, viewed through a haze of superstition as beastial in the most negative sense, were thus regarded as mechanical in behavior.

Seeds for a more realistic philosophy were sown during the Age of Exploration when sailors such as Columbus and Magellan began redrawing world maps. In the sixteenth century a group that came to be known as naturalists began tagging along on exploratory voyages. Well-educated and usually from well-to-do families, they were considered—by professional scholars and sailors alike—to be playboys, not to be taken seriously. Although their journals were suspect in the scholarly realm, this new breed began to record previously unknown species of animals and plants from around the globe and to examine relationships in nature.

Midway through the nineteenth century the naturalist movement

6

found its most explosive expression in the unlikely person of a mild-mannered young Englishman named Charles Darwin. *Origin of Species* may be his most famous work, but his writings also include a publication that pioneered much of behavioral science: *The Expression of the Emotions in Man and Animal*. In his travels around South America aboard the HMS *Beagle* Darwin found evidence that all the components of nature—animal, vegetable, mineral—changed repeatedly throughout time, as if constantly seeking a better way. "The survival of the fittest," he called it. Behavior was as much a part of the survival mechanism as physical form when plants and animals adapted to changing environments.

The surviving organisms passed along a heritage of drives that stimulated survival behavior and Darwin recognized that the drives could alter as conditions fluctuated. The British naturalist thus breathed new life into the concept propounded centuries earlier by Aristotle—instinct. Being the genius he was, Darwin also realized that animal behavior resulted from a complicated interplay of forces, that learning and emotion were as influential as instinctive drives.

Darwin's revolutionary writings ignited additional revolutions—and sometimes, scientific silliness—during the late nineteenth and early twentieth centuries. Early in this century a group referred to as comparative psychologists turned back the clock. Or at least slowed it down. Comparative psychologists had little use for the concept of instinct, believing instead that various stimuli from the environment triggered behavior. Learning was the key.

With that orientation—and a somewhat subjective passion for clinical objectivity—their investigation of behavior was restricted to laboratory work in which they created and manipulated environments. The anecdotal approach of the field biologist was viewed with considerable disdain by the comparative psychologists. Control was paramount for objectivity's sake and they preferred to push buttons and set off reactions rather than to wait and see what developed.

One of the pioneers in this brand of research, the American, E. L. Thorndike, devised some of the earliest problem boxes, a laboratory method of quantifying the abilities of different species to learn. The Nobel prize–winning Russian scientist, I. P. Pavlov, conditioned dogs to salivate to neutral stimuli—the sound of bells. Another American, J. B. Watson, devoted much of his effort to stimulating animals to responses that differed from their standard behavioral repertoire. Thus he modified the behavior of cats, conditioning them to run from rats. Through such experiments Watson concluded that negative rewards—punishment, that is—had a greater impact than positive reinforcement.

Your average dog does not drool when it hears bells ringing but much of the comparative psychologists' experimentation did advance scientific knowledge of animal—and human—organisms. It also bore only a tenuous relationship to the ways in which animals behave in nature.

Fortunately, other scientists in Europe and North America were beginning to explore the natural route during the 1920s. These ethological pioneers stressed the importance of instinct and of observing behavior under natural conditions. Among other things they considered the phenomenon of imprinting, a concept developed by D. A. Spalding late in the nineteenth century. Spalding found that newly hatched chicks would follow the first thing they saw that moved, be it chicken or human. His successors observed the same thing in geese, ducks, and a variety of other animals, and they examined the influence of imprinting on adult behavior.

Seeds for an infant science. Finally, in the 1930s, a new group of zoologists emerged to spark the rapid growth of the modern science of ethology. A great many men and women made important contributions during this era but three stand out as a kind of ethological trinity: the Austrians Konrad Lorenz and Karl Von Frisch and a Dutchman, Nikolaas Tinbergen. All have written classics in the literature of animal behavior and, in 1973, these innovative scientists were awarded the first Nobel laureates in ethology.

Perhaps the best known because of his numerous popular books as well as scientific volumes, Konrad Lorenz was originally attracted to the field by the writing of his predecessors on imprinting. Lorenz expanded greatly on that work and on the understanding of instinctive behavior generally. His studies of aggression—in humans as well as animals—set off considerable controversy. More often than not, the bearded, grandfatherly Lorenz is pictured trailing a gaggle of goslings that regard him as mother. This is due not only to imprinting but to Lorenz's ability to learn animal language literally. His desire to relate to animals on their terms, rather than a human's, has enabled him to "converse" with monkeys, dogs, ducks, geese, shrews, and many other wild creatures.

Karl Von Frisch first jostled conventional thinking by demonstrating that honeybees could see color. Why else, he reasoned, would flowers have such bright colors? (Reasonable or not, Von Frisch still had to document it, testing the bees with various color cards.) He went on to decode the "dance of the bees," in which these social insects use body movements to inform other members as to the direction and distance of a source of honey.

In his youth Niko Tinbergen watched and wondered how, when a swarm of wasps returns to the nest, each individual automatically heads for its own burrow without confusion. Such curiosity led to a series of classic studies, such as the one conducted on a small fish called the stickleback. The male, having constructed a grassy nest on a stream bed and having lured one or more female sticklebacks to it, then hovers over the eggs laid by his partner(s) and fans them with his fins. Dr. Tinbergen determined that the little fish did so to aerate the eggs. Without that instinctive response the young would not hatch.

As the decades of the twentieth century passed, these gentlemen and a growing number of colleagues documented the life-styles of a great many other species. World War II naturally stifled field research, except for what could be done in backyards or nearby forests and meadows. But during the postwar decades, field studies—in part, fueled by wartime technology—blossomed, providing new insights that thrilled the scientific community and lay public alike.

Among the rush of landmark field studies conducted during this era, mostly by American and British zoologists, several stand out. George Schaller unraveled many of the mysteries of lion society and the predatory existence of those great cats in Tanzania's Serengeti National Park. Other Schaller projects unveiled dramatic new pictures of mountain gorillas, tigers, and Asian mountain sheep. More recently Dian Fossey added to the mountain gorilla portrait during a long-range study in which she developed amazing rapport with those enormously powerful yet gentle apes. Jane Goodall continues to uncover new surprises in chimpanzee society, finding that this appealing ape exhibits some of the less ingratiating and violent traits of human civilization.

A Dutch scientist, Hans Kruuk, provided the much maligned spotted hyena with a whole new image: that of a skillful predator, not merely the cringing scavenger with disgusting (to people) habits. L. David Mech illuminated the complex behavior and ecological role of another highly social predator, the wolf. Roger Payne recorded and identified songs from several whale species, traced changes in their music over long periods, and speculated about song as a possible means of communication among cetaceans. Iain Douglas-Hamilton deltailed the delicate interrelationships of African elephant society and captured the individual personalities of these highly civilized beasts.

Although birds are sometimes more difficult to study, many being so much in motion high above the ground, they have not been neglected. Richard Penney, for instance, braved subzero temperatures to learn how penguins have adapted behavior—courtship, mating, reproduction, parental care, and the like—to the frigid, barren Antarctic.

How behaviorists behave. The basic tools of all these people in the bush remains paper and pencil. Hour after hour, day after day, weeks and months on end, they record observations and jot various arcane symbols in rumpled, sometimes soggy, notebooks. Sometimes they depend on tape recorders (so they can make notes without taking their eyes off the animal). Every sniff, every kick, nearly every flutter of an animal's eyelash. From endless details, the researcher pieces together behavioral patterns.

Behavioral research is almost never glamorous. Sometimes it becomes dangerous, due to climate or terrain or human revolutionaries and not

10

because of savage beasts. More often than not it is boring. George Schaller once commented: "A Serengeti lion sleeps twenty-one hours a day on the average, a hoofed animal spends ten hours a day or more eating grass. You spend hours and hours waiting for something to happen."

Thanks to late twentieth-century technology, contemporary behaviorists can rely on more than pencil and pad and brain power to assist them when something does happen. High-powered binoculars, sophisticated cameras, and long-distance lenses—all of them superior to what was available decades earlier—are standard equipment. Many researchers also employ movie cameras to capture the action. Likewise tape recorders.

Sometimes things can be made to happen. Without fouling up natural responses, that is. Researchers often use tape recorders to reproduce the sound of the species under scrutiny, then watch the reaction of others of its kind. Or the tape-recorded voice may provoke a secretive creature to reveal itself—say, in order to defend a territory—so that it can be observed, not merely listened to. Very handy technique in dark, deep, dank rain forests.

Among the biggest boons to behavioral research is a combination of transistorized electronics and pharmaceutical progress. Behaviorist sharpshooters now use air guns to dart their subjects with projectiles that explode on impact, injecting a tranquilizing drug. These airborne knockout drops anesthetize the animal harmlessly and for a long enough period that the biologist can safely attach a small, almost weightless plastic collar that contains a miniature radio transmitter. While the animal is still unconscious, the researcher has an opportunity to gather important vital statistics: weight, length, health, notable physical characteristics, dental condition, and so on. Once the subject revives it becomes a sort of walking radio station, broadcasting its whereabouts and some of its activities even when it cannot be seen.

The airplane has proved valuable and not merely for ferrying investigators to remote outposts. By flying transect patterns across a given area the observer can census wildlife populations below, often picking up individual animals that, obscured by vegetation, would be "invisible" on the ground. The researcher confirms this aerial survey with a second tabulation at ground level.

Computer technology has also gotten involved. After a long period of collecting data, it is comforting to have a friendly, beeping, flashing piece of hardware back at the university to help analyze all those bits of information.

Gadgetry has not replaced ingenuity, however. When detailing the affairs of animals it is vital to be able to identify individuals. To human eyes, one member of a species may look pretty much like another of the same age and sex. Especially at the distances that animals insist upon between themselves and observers. One enterprising behaviorist, Judith Rudnai, while investigating lions in Kenya, realized that each member of the pride has its own distinct pattern of spots around its muzzle—where the whiskers are. So she created a system of index cards showing a generic lion face on which she sketched the whisker spot pattern of each individual, as well as other identifying features such as rips or notches in ears and missing teeth. Sort of like a file of fingerprints or "mug shots."

Many of the species still unstudied present special problems. Lots of zoologists would like to study snow leopards. But those beautiful, very secretive felines inhabit the high-altitude slopes of the Himalayas, an extremely harsh and vast landscape. Just getting there requires a monumental effort. Even residents of the region hardly ever see snow leopards. Only paw prints in the snow.

Smaller cats—ocelots, servals, caracals, margays, Pallas's cats—have their own built-in barriers to research. They are as described: small. Their nocturnal lifestyle, together with the fact that a great many of these cats inhabit dense tropical rain forests, make it darn near impossible to see them.

Yet the matter is not hopeless. Researchers have had some success studying nocturnal predators on the African savanna with another by-product of wartime technology: the image intensifier. Once top secret equipment, the "sniper scopes" permit observations of animal habits—instead of the movements of enemy soldiers—after dark.

Ethology brings a new slant on survival. The growth of behavioral research has value far beyond the expansion of human knowledge. It could mean survival for the animals. For many of them, anyway. After centuries of human misunderstanding, indifference, superstition, positively loony-viewpoints, and, let's face it, persecution of wild creatures, mankind is now attempting to make amends. Whether or not we can reverse the trend toward extinction that threatens almost all wildlife seems questionable. If the reversal can be accomplished, the data collected by field biologists will be one of the primary weapons.

As human populations mushroom and wilderness disappears, space for animals dwindles as well. Soon, specifically designated refuges such as national parks, will be the only places on earth left for wildlife.

To create preserves properly we must understand the animals' requirements. Any old piece of land that no one else wants won't do. Which is where the behaviorist comes in. The researchers are telling us the type of habitat necessary; the food of the species in question; how they obtain it; whether they are residents or migrants and, if the latter, the patterns of their travels; the nature of their societies; how they communicate; their courtship and mating habits; how they rear their young; and other essential information.

I wish the behavioral folk success, for it seems to me a profound tragedy to lose these animals just as we are beginning to get to know them.

Lowland Gorilla

1 ❖ *Why does a gorilla beat its chest?*

That depends. On the gorilla and the situation. In some instances, it may be just what it seems: a statement of defiance toward a challenging rival or an intruder—while sizing up the situation. Or, loosely translated: "I'm one tough ape, and you'd better not press your luck, because I'm not scared!"

In order to deliver a similar but more serious, less equivocal message, a gorilla may use chest-beating as a threat, clearly intending to intimidate and drive away something or someone whose presence constitutes a potential danger. The menace might be another troop of gorillas, encountered while foraging for food, or a human, even one without a gun. On such occasions the troop leader, usually a huge silverbacked male, will rise and beat his chest to issue the warning. He drums quite rapidly, and then usually explodes into a roaring charge, sounding very much like a chorus of all the demons in Hell.

Yet in reality, gorillas (whose scientific name is *gorilla gorilla*) are pussycats. The most aggressive charge rarely results in serious physical combat. Even human observers—if their grit holds out against a shrieking Gargantua bearing down on them—have found repeatedly that the challenging gorilla will stop short of violence. It's somewhat akin to the message of a marshal who fires his six-gun over an outlaw's head: Get out of town by sundown or draw and take the consequences.

Sometimes chest-beating signifies the relief of tension that might occur after a danger or challenge has passed—"Hey! I'm okay!" A little chest-beating is one thing, but a gorilla does not stage a victory celebration, drumming a ferocious tattoo on his chest while shaking the trees with a "Lord of the Jungle" victory cheer after cracking an op-

15

ponent's spine. That sort of thing happens only in "Tarzan" comics and movies.

Since gorillas forage for food over extensive, thickly forested areas, they are not always in visual contact. Chest-beating may then be used to signal location, as when the leader calls his troop together. Or it may alert other unseen gorillas feeding in the same area, thereby avoiding conflict.

Defense or orientation, pounding on the chest is not strictly a machismo declaration. Females do it as well, although with less frequency. So do youngsters during playful brawls.

Gorillas, especially youthful ones, also beat their chests purely as an expression of high spirits. The beat is much slower than when they threaten. If, on a sunny, summer day, you visit a zoo that has outdoor ape exhibits, you may well see a young male tilt his head back into the warm light and thump his chest. While serious students of behavior wisely avoid investing animals with human emotions—that's called "anthropomorphism"—there can be no doubt this gorilla feels good.

Contrary to what Hollywood producers or comic strip artists would have you believe, gorillas beat their chests with the palms of their hands open and slightly cupped, not with doubled-up fists. Thus they produce a staccato series of hollow pops—like the noise made by a stopper pried from a bottle. It appears that the apes have learned that the cupped-palm method generates a louder noise. Gorillas are often smarter than some Hollywood producers.

2 ❖ Why do rhinos take mud baths?

Because it feels terrific. All five species of rhinoceros remaining on earth live in very hot, tropical regions of Africa and Asia. All of them seek out areas that remain muddy most of the time—perhaps the edges of a swamp, a spot with poor drainage. And they wallow in it, rolling and flopping about in the ooze with great abandon. The place, which they visit at every available opportunity, is called a wallow. Which is

Indian Rhino

why rhinos, whether you see them in zoos or in photos, always seem to be caked with clay.

As noted, mud is a great comfort to them. It's cooling. It adds a kind of protective layer against the sun (though sunburn is an unlikely possibility).

Mud prevents irritating itching and burning—without the cost of a patent remedy—because it adds a barrier that prevents at least some biting insects and parasites from nibbling at the rhino's hide, which is more tender than it appears.

Elephants (both *Elephas maximus* and *Loxodonta africana*) display a similar inclination toward mud for essentially the same reasons. If they have access to a muddy wallow large enough to accommodate their bulk, they will plunge in. If not, they pick up earth with their trunks and spray it over themselves, a sort of dust shower.

3 ❖ *Why do geese mate for life?*

To survive, animals must be very practical. The lifetime fidelity of gander and goose has more to do with pragmatism than with romance. The nesting grounds for many of the world's species of geese—Canada, snow, bar-headed, gray lag, and so on—are above the Arctic Circle. To reach home base, the geese must migrate several thousand miles. The birds can't rush the departure date because weather at their destination would make life impossible for early arrivals.

Once there, pairs of geese get down to no-nonsense breeding: they mate, lay eggs, and hatch them as rapidly as nature will permit. The goslings must develop to the point where they can fly, a process that requires roughly eight weeks, depending on the species. It is essential that the new generation be airborne for the trip south; frigid weather will soon return, wiping out food supplies.

Time is precious to survival: If the geese also had to seek new mates each year, they would never make it. Mate selection is itself a time-consuming activity. Hence, the geese form permanent pair-bonds, the zoologists' term for such a "marriage." (Pair-bond refers to any union formed for the purpose of mating; it may last only for days, weeks, months, or even for life, as with the geese.)

To further avoid wasting time, geese perform much of their courtship ritual, and renewal of bonds, in southern latitudes prior to migration. When they land in the Arctic, they are "ready."

While all geese, even the domestic varieties, form lifelong pairs, not all of them migrate to nest in the Arctic. The néné, or Hawaiian goose (*Branta sandvicensis*) stays right at home in the Tropics, unpressured by climate. However, the néné is fairly close kin to the Canada goose

18

(*Branta canadensis*). Their common ancestor was a pair-bonder out of necessity and that trait stuck with the Hawaiian branch of the family. (Nénés may not spend holidays in the Arctic, but they engage in their own brand of cliff-hanging by nesting on the slopes of active volcanoes.) Although the desirability of staying put on the islands may seem obvious to anyone who has read a Hawaiian travel brochure, it is not known exactly why nénés abandoned the practice of migration. For that matter, no one knows for certain why geese chose to nest within the Arctic Circle. One possibility is that sites were established—and programmed into the genes of the geese—eons ago when weather patterns were different; the Arctic climate was milder, more hospitable.

Permanent pair-bonding is not unique to geese. Some eagles, storks, hawks, all cranes, and many other birds do it—for many of the same reasons as the geese. It is common mostly to large species.

Among the smaller species, include the Adélie penguin (*Psygosceles adeliae*), whose breeding grounds lie within 800 miles of the South Pole. Male and female birds are separated from each other and at sea for seven months of the year. Yet many mates follow a "same time next year" routine. As many as eighty percent of the pairs are reunited when breeding season arrives. (More research is necessary to determine whether they actually form permanent pairs.) This bonded majority demonstrates the wisdom of a pair-bond arrangement in that kind of

Canada Geese

sub-zero neighborhood. They are much better able to take advantage of the abbreviated breeding season in the Antarctic. Such pairs produce and raise viable offspring at a much higher rate than those that decline to commit themselves to return engagements.

4 ❖ *Why do cranes dance?*

If they didn't, there would be no crane chicks every year. Cranes, the family *Gruidae,* form permanent pair-bonds, and dancing is a vital aspect of their courtship and mating ritual.

For young, just-maturing cranes that have never mated, the ceremony is necessary to the creation of a bond. Among already mated pairs, dancing reinforces the established union—a sort of annual renewal of vows.

Internally, these rites synchronize the male and female sexually. Thus, when they arrive at their breeding grounds, the male will have viable sperm ready to fertilize his mate's developing eggs. Such coordination is particularly crucial for those species whose breeding grounds lie near the Arctic Circle where time available for producing the next generation is quite limited.

Dr. George Archibald, whose International Crane Foundation is dedicated to preserving these birds, goes dancing with cranes all the time for just that reason. Because cranes are among the most endangered of all birds, Dr. Archibald is breeding them through artificial insemination whenever he can't put together a properly mating pair. It does no good to inject semen if the female is not synchronized; there will be no fertile eggs unless the ancient rites are observed. Dr. A. and his partner dance for survival.

"Dance floors" are created wherever cranes flock. Early in the morning, before they fly off to feeding sites and again at dusk when they return, birds will repeat the ritual several times. All fifteen species of

White-naped Crane

crane do virtually the same steps, though there may be minor variations.

They do a number that goes like this: With wings outstretched, male and female begin circling each other, striding with long, quick steps. They bow their heads repeatedly, occasionally flinging twigs or earth into the air. Periodically they will erupt with a leap of several feet straight up. They may conclude with a long side-by-side run, flapping their wings stiffly so they are sometimes lifted from the ground. In a furious finish, the birds bring their heads low between their legs and flap their wings wildly. As the wings close, they snap their heads upward and back toward the middle of their backs, then return, stopping abruptly in the normally erect, stately crane pose. *Saturday Night Fever* it may not be, but it is highly energetic—and utterly serious, no matter how funny it may appear.

5 ❖ *Why do wolves howl?*

The extremely intelligent, highly social wolf (*Canis lupus*) has developed one of the more complex communication systems in the animal kingdom. Much of it is an elaborate "body language." Among an equally rich repertoire of vocalizations, the howl is probably the most familiar—just because of legend.

Howling may play a role in several situations. Perhaps the most important relates to the pack's territory, where the animals have staked out exclusive hunting rights. Just as a pack does not welcome other wolves into the territory, they are equally wary of invading someone else's turf. Surprise attacks will probably provoke mayhem.

Normally, wolves, as individuals or packs, prefer to avoid fighting. It's wasteful. They need their strength for basic survival. So they howl. If the neighboring pack is nearby it will answer, alerting the first bunch that they are getting too close for the comfort of all concerned.

Sometimes territories overlap. So long as two packs aren't simultaneously sharing the area, it's no problem. The important factor is to maintain an appropriate—read safe—distance.

This same sort of territorial distancing is rather common in the animal kingdom: It's a major reason why lions roar, gibbons hoot, howler monkeys howl, and birds of many species sing.

Because territories, depending on locale, climate, size of food supply, etc., can extend over several square miles, individual pack members also howl to keep in touch with each other, to signal their positions when they are separated. Makes for more efficient hunting and social contact in general. Since wolves do much of their hunting at night when they cannot see as well, communicating by howling becomes even more essential, both for avoiding conflict and maintaining contact.

Tundra Wolves

It also leads to mythology: the image of the lonely wolf, or his distant descendant, your good ole hound dog, baying at a full moon. The howl has a mournful, plaintive ring to human ears. Until rather recently, people assumed loneliness was the cause. The moon is strictly coincidental. Wolves also howl on nights when there is no moon. Maybe more. There's less light.

Long ago, people searching for explanations connected howling wolves with full moons, then carried the notion one step further to accommodate the werewolf, a fiction that was, itself, born of a need to find reasons or fix blame for mysterious, frightening events. The fact is, there are *very* few documented cases of bona fide wolves attacking or killing people. The wolf, one of the world's most intelligent and socially sophisticated animals, has, for centuries, also been one of the most maligned by mythology. As a result it has been one of the most persecuted of creatures and today it is designated as an endangered species throughout most of its range.

6 ❖ *Why do crocodile mothers swallow their babies?*

Doting mom that she is, she's taking the kids to the beach. Considering the crocodile's bad press, that may surprise you. Not many people associate the warmth and tender loving care of maternity with a ten-foot-long, scaly-skinned reptile owning the most awesome set of dentures this side of the shark family. Thanks to in-depth studies, such as the investigation of the Nile crocodile (*Crocodylus nilocticus*) by South African game warden Anthony Pooley, these refugees from the Age of Dinosaurs are beginning to upgrade their image. Slightly.

Having been courted and mated, the crocodile mother-to-be removes herself to land, some distance from the waters of sexual rendezvous. She hollows a hole eight-to-twelve-inches deep in the ground, deposits her clutch of eggs within, then covers them with earth, patting it down with her body and tail. Now she takes up guard duty, rarely leaving the nest.

During the incubation period of some eighty-four to ninety days, the fiery African sun bakes the soil covering the nest into a clay nearly as hard as rock. When little crocodiles begin hatching underground, they find escape darn near impossible. Frustration elicits the hatchlings' cries for help: a chorus of yelps, squawks, and croaks that stimulate a response in the mother. She rips open the nest.

As the youngsters clamber upward, the adult catches each one firmly yet gently between her teeth. She seems to gulp and the hatchling drops out of sight. One after another they are snatched up only to vanish into the great tooth-lined gap between her jaws. A few of the young walk right in of their own accord and disappear.

Some eggs are slow to hatch, or the occupants can't quite make it on

24

their own. Grasping an egg with jaws powerful enough to crush the leg of an ox, the mother cracks the brittle shell. The inner skin she punctures with her fearsome teeth, handling the operation with a deftness and delicacy that would do a human mother proud, and releases another babe.

Meanwhile, back in the abyss, the "swallowed" hatchlings are not digesting in their mother's stomach. They are nestled cozily amongst their kin, some even asleep, inside mother's gular pouch, the rather elastic skin stretching across the lower jawbone. Research suggests that its capacity for expansion is sufficient to hold the female's entire brood, perhaps twenty or more.

Once everyone is aboard, the mother, loaded pouch drooping and

Nile Crocodile

swaying, trundles toward the water's edge. Slipping into the pool, she opens her jaws and releases her progeny into the water.

And that is the whole point of the exercise: help them get into the water. Nests are sometimes located hundreds of yards away from water, a precaution against flooding of the nest. Lacking the navigational talents of baby turtles, the little crocodiles would probably fan out willy-nilly, perhaps never finding the water where there is food, as well as other essentials for survival.

Mama crocodile then establishes a sort of nursery pool in which she guards her brood vigilantly for about six months. Still, it takes several years and a few feet of growth before these youngsters reach the top of the predator pile. During that time some will become the victims of hawks, herons, storks, otters, monitor lizards, and other skillful hunters. But when they need help during the earliest, bumpiest stages of life, they've got it. Gently. With endless patience. Without complaint. After all, what are mothers for?

7 ❖ Why do raccoons wash their food?

Sanitation is not the intention. Raccoons (*Procyon lotor*) aren't washing food at all but prospecting for it. Using what appears to be a scrubbing action, the animals probe and sift the sand and gravel of a streambed to find crayfish, snails, mussels—crustaceans in general. Once they find them, they waste no time on preliminaries.

The illusion of washing is enhanced by the fact that the raccoons' fingerlike paws are extremely nimble and touch-oriented; they approach the human hand in dexterity and sensitivity.

Something more like actual washing occurred with a well-studied troop of Japanese macaques (*Macaca fuscata*) commonly called "snow monkeys," which lived near the ocean. To lure the monkeys from the forest so their behavior might be observed more easily in an open space, researchers placed potatoes and wheat on the beach. The monkeys accepted and dug in.

One of the females soon took to washing her sandy potatoes in the surf. Within a fairly short time other members of the band were dunking their spuds, too. It was simply a demonstration of simian intelligence. Observations indicate that, almost certainly, the salt water not only removes sand, it makes the potatoes taste better. The monkeys also learned that when they threw the wheat on the water, the chaff separated from the kernels (as did the sand), making it easier to get at the good stuff.

Apparently the initial step was an accidental one, but the pioneering female realized she was on to a good thing, and the others bought the idea. Washing, perhaps, but monkeys aren't compulsive about cleanliness. They're too intelligent.

Raccoon

8 ❖ *Do chimpanzees really use tools?*

They not only use tools, they invent them. Dr. Jane Goodall brought this phenomenon to the world's attention. To the chimpanzees (*Pan troglodytes*) termites are a delicacy. But, in their hard, earthen mounds laced with intricate networks of tunnels, the insects are not easily procured. Dr. Goodall learned that a very simple tool makes it possible for chimpanzees to go termite fishing. The chimp simply scrapes away the surface of the nest with a finger, then inserts a long stem of grass—the tool. Almost instantly termites react defensively and grab at the intruding element. The chimpanzee retrieves the tool with termites dangling from it and nibbles them off, like a kid with a lollipop. Chimps have also been known to use rocks to crack open nuts. Hunger is a great motivator for intellectual development.

Dr. Goodall even observed chimps stripping leaves from twigs to use as fishing rods. They were thus modifying an instrument to create a tool rather than employing it as is. It's a rather unsophisticated tool and somewhat distant from the accomplishments of even the most primitive humans, but it is definitely tool-making—and in the right direction.

The same intellectual gifts are operative in the making of chimpanzee sponges. The animal will grasp a bunch of leaves, chew them, and roll them into a ball. It plunks the leaf sponge into tree hollows and other places where water collects. When the leaves are soaked the chimp retrieves the sponge and squeezes the liquid into its mouth.

Tool-using is not a chimpanzee exclusive. Sea otters (*Enhydra lutris*), though limited in their tool kit, probably spend more time at such activity than any other animal. Adrift on its back in offshore currents, an otter holds a tasty but solidly sealed shellfish between its front paws. With a burst of energy, the animal bashes the shell down against a rock propped on its chest. After a rapid-fire series of whacks, the shell cracks open and dinner's on: clam, mussel, sea urchin, or that delicacy, abalone.

That course over, the otter, assuming it is still hungry, dives down to pluck another mollusk from its undersea garden. Occasionally otters also use their stone "mallets" to knock tougher, larger shellfish loose from the bottom of the ocean.

Birds are tool-users, too. On the Galapagos Islands, the woodpecker finch (*Camarhynchus pallidus*) will grasp a twig or cactus spine with its bill, then probe inside trees and pry out grubs and other insects.

The northern (or great gray) shrike (*Lanius excubitor*) stores its insect prey by impaling the bugs on thorny bushes or depositing them in the forks of tree branches. Egyptian vultures (*Neophron percnopterus*) relish ostrich eggs, but the shells are too thick for the vultures to crack open by pecking. So they throw rocks. Clutching a stone with its beak, the vulture rears its head back and fires at the egg. Once the shell has been bombarded repeatedly—the vultures miss about fifty percent of their shots—it breaks, and the bird dines on the contents.

In Australia, the male satin bowerbird (*Ptilonorhynchus violaceus*) constructs a basketlike bower—a remarkably intricate weaving job for a bird—in which he dances to court a female. Not content with building, he decorates with spots of color here and there. He is especially fond of bits of blue broken glass. Up to this point the only tool he has used is his bill. He also "paints" the bower with berry juices and fruit pulp, his "brush"—more like a sponge, really—being a wad of fibrous bark from which he squeezes the juice/paint.

Chimpanzees and other anthropoid apes had demonstrated their tool-using gifts in laboratories long before Dr. Goodall or anyone else realized they did this sort of thing on their own. A series of classic experiments demonstrated that a chimp could fashion tools of a sort to obtain bananas placed outside the cage or hung from a high ceiling. To extend its reach beyond the bars the animal connected several rods and pulled the bananas within grabbing range. By stacking several

Chimpanzee

boxes it improvised a sort of ladder that allowed the chimp to claim its ceiling-high reward.

Animals have also been known to bring their ingenuity to bear on the human world—often in a very disconcerting manner. Orangutans are notorious for doing so. These Indonesian apes not only possess considerable intelligence and manual dexterity, they exhibit the patience required of an adept problem-solver.

Nowhere has this been exemplified better than by a wily male orang at the Henry Doorly Zoo in Omaha, Nebraska. Several years back keepers at the primate house were surprised one morning when they

30

encountered this animal roaming freely in the corridor behind the exhibits (rather than inside his cage where he should have been). No damage was done, and the animal was enticed back into his quarters and locked in. Morning after morning, keepers had no sooner punched in than they would open the door to find this red-haired rascal on the prowl in what was supposed to be the keepers' work area. Each night security was checked and double-checked—to no avail. There was no evidence of human mischief but no clues to a break-out strategy either.

Naturally the staff took to watching their anthropoid Houdini much more closely. Finally someone found the key—literally. It seems the ape had acquired a small piece of wire which, until he thought no one was looking, he hid inside his mouth. And, each evening, when the zoo crew departed, he simply picked the lock of his cage with his little wire tool. It is not the only instance of escape artistry among orangutans, and zoo officials in Omaha swear the story is not animal apochrypha.

Why all the fuss about tool-using and making? Because these animals (and there are numerous other examples) have learned to use an object, sometimes modifying it, that allows them to accomplish tasks beyond the limits of their natural physical endowments. They have stretched their normal physical, and sometimes mental, capabilities. It's also because, only a few years ago, the scientific community agreed that one characteristic that separated man from all other animals was that humans made and used tools. We no longer have a patent on tools, even though one may scoff at the crudeness of animal tools. We had to start somewhere, too.

9 ❖ Why do birds sing?

Some definitions are in order. To qualify as song, the sound must be a fairly complex combination of a substantial variety of musical notes and changes of key. A bird strings the notes together in series, related to each other, and with regular rhythmic patterning, so that they form a clearly recognizable sequence. Melody, if you will. A "peep" is not a song.

Three-wattled Bell Bird

Secondly, not all of the more than 9,000 bird species sing, though a great many do. Song is pretty much restricted to the Oscines, a subdivision of the Passerines (perching birds), largest of the bird orders. The suborder of Oscines—we call them songbirds—totals nearly 4,000 species. They include such familiar songsters as larks, wrens, mockingbirds, warblers, and orioles.

This is not to say that the rest of avian society is mute. To the contrary they are a noisy lot—honking, squawking, clucking, quacking, whistling, hooting, and so on, but they are not singers of songs.

In a high proportion of songbird species, only the male possesses the gift of melody. Moreover, that talent has sexual roots. Hormones, for the most part, start the music, getting the birds in tune for the annual reproductive cycle. Songbirds use their melodies to map out, and then defend, territories. Sometimes singing substitutes for feathered fighting between two males contesting a territory—a sort of battle of the singers.

While shooing other males away, the bird is, through song, simultaneously suing for a mate, trying to woo an unattached female as surely as a love-smitten balladeer strumming his guitar beneath a damsel's window. It is thought that once the birds are mated, singing reinforces and upholds the pair-bond they have established. Probably it also is an important factor in reproductive success, helping to synchronize the birds' sexual cycles during the early stages of their "relationship."

Aside from these practical virtues, there is strong scientific evidence that birds sing just because they are enjoying themselves. Jubilant and utterly irresponsible. Moreover, some birds—including certain nightingales and blackbirds, probably many more—are even "composers." They spontaneously recombine musical phrases they have sung before to "write" new songs.

If a peep is not a song, it is probably a call note. Calling is distinguished from singing by the fact that it is usually restricted to one or two notes, four or five at the maximum. Call notes have little to do with sex; they coordinate behavior among other members of the species. A call may, for example, be an alarm: "Hawk overhead at four o'clock! Hide!" Calling also helps to orchestrate such activities as flocking, migration, and feeding.

Melody aside, the entire matter of animal communication has become a branch of behavioral study unto itself—an enormously complex one. One of the more intriguing aspects appears in a theory proposed by Dr. Eugene S. Morton, a research zoologist at the National Zoo in Washington, D.C. Reporting in 1980, Dr. Morton concluded that, among those animals that vocalize (some, like salamanders, are mute), a high percentage of them use the same three basic sounds to express themselves. Makes no difference whether it's a rhinoceros or a wren. They use a common language.

Dr. Morton classifies the basics as "growl" (for aggressive or hostile circumstances), "whine" (to indicate friendly intentions or appeasement), and "bark" (as a means of attracting attention or an indication of indecisiveness). Yes, the ornithologist assures us, wrens do growl.

His evidence lies in sonagrams of an extensive repertoire of animal sounds. An instrument called a sonograph analyzes the sounds and translates them into a picture or graph that tracks frequency and pitch changes within a specific time frame. Despite what the human ear hears, the sonagrams show that elephants and eagles and beagles make the same sounds in comparable situations.

What is more, Dr. Morton includes people among the creatures that depend on growling, whining, and barking for basic communication. It isn't only the words we use; in fact, words may be intended as camouflage for feelings revealed by tone of voice. If Dr. Morton's theory proves out—and he has impressive data—we may all turn out to be "birds of a feather."

10 ❖ *How do birds learn to sing?*

Some song they inherit, some they learn from other birds, but not necessarily their parents.

Most of what is known about birdsong was learned from Dr. Peter Marler's studies of the European chaffinch (*Fringilla coelebs*). In laboratory studies at Rockefeller University in New York City, Marler demonstrated that babies taken from the nest and hand-raised in isolation from every other bird, will emit only the rudiments of the song of their species. Since this very simple song is fairly undistinguished to the human ear, researchers use sound spectrographs to make "pictures" of it and compare that song with the fully developed melody of the adult chaffinch. The graph of the isolated chick song reveals that portion of the species singing that is innate.

A series of further studies demonstrated additional evidence of avian musical instruction. If several of those same isolated chicks were grouped together, yet isolated from all other birds, for about ten months, they were able to develop much more complex melodies by vocally stimulating each other to sing and through imitation. However, the songs they created bore little or no resemblance to the normal song of wild chaffinches.

It's a different story when the birds have the opportunity to spend their formative early months listening to the singing of mature, experienced males. Juveniles that were trapped during the first autumn after

Mossy-throated Bell Bird

hatching were also raised in laboratory isolation until the following summer. Their songs were nearly normal, although not quite as complex as the songs of wild cousins.

When juveniles of this age were placed in community groups rather than solitary confinement so they could hear only each other, they tended to produce a rather uniform song. Individual variation is dulled by copycatting. They have no opportunity to learn that other musical possibilities may be explored.

Song, then, seems to come in stages. The basics are inborn. During early weeks of life the youngsters elaborate on that by learning other aspects of the species song from male parents or others. It is not until they reach their first breeding season when, stimulated by the musical "inventiveness" of their competitors, they add the finishing touches. In the bird world, it takes a while before a song is born. This final stage even produces dialects that may differ significantly from one locality to another, even though it's the same basic song.

Singing comes much more easily to some other members of the animal kingdom. The first time a cricket chirps, it produces the simple "song" of its species fully developed. The signal is born into the cricket, and it never varies. The insects must acquire their songs by inheritance because, in nearly all species, all the ancestors have passed away months before. Crickets have no teachers, nobody to listen to except their own generation.

11 ❖ *Do birds ever sing duets?*

In many songbird species, females do not sing. So much for duets in that group.

On the minority side, females of some species do sing, and some of them even join their mates in duets. Motmots and some ovenbirds, for instance, sing in pairs. Usually such duos occur during courtship and when they are reinforcing the pair-bond.

Most of the species thus inclined live in thickly wooded areas, such as tropical rain forest or dense scrub. That kind of habitat often makes it difficult for a pair to remain in visual contact. It is rather vital that they don't lose each other as the survival of the species depends on it. They must mate, nest, lay eggs, raise young.

So far as can be determined, no birds are singing two-part harmony, but some species are joining in a rather spectacular type of duetting called antiphonal singing. This special group includes some African shrikes, barbets, and Central American wrens. Instead of singing simultaneously, the male and female alternate musical phrases—often quite different ones. Their timing is so incredibly precise that, unless you are positioned so you can see them, you would swear that a single bird is singing.

Even non-songbirds perform duets. For example, cranes, whose raucous bugling sounds anything but musical, join in a unison call. A mated pair snap their heads back and, with beaks pointed skyward, the male trumpets low-frequency notes while the female calls with high-frequency tones. Their sound—nature's own stereo—is so perfectly synchronized it seems to come from a single bird. Such duetting helps to maintain the pair-bond, coordinate their sexual states, and occasionally, serves as a territorial threat to drive other cranes away.

36

Lesson's Motmot

12 ❖ *Why does a mockingbird mock?*

Everyone seems to agree that members of this family definitely imitate other bird families. Ornithologists, however, continue to debate about how much of their song is deliberate mimicry.

The mockingbird's reputation stems from its versatility. Though it may repeat notes, the pattern of its singing is far less rigid than that of other songbirds, and it may continue for a relatively long time.

Research has shown that, for most mockingbird species (the genus *Mimus*), imitation is strictly coincidental, not intentional. Because of the great variety and complexity of the mockingbird's song, it is bound to hit on notes that copy, or at least suggest, the vocalizations of another species. The longer and more varied the mockingbird's song, the more easily people assume they are hearing another bird.

If, for example, you know there is a cardinal nesting in your neighborhood and you are familiar with its song, you are sure to catch the local mockingbird repeating the cardinal's song. Chances are, it is purely fortuitous. One research study indicated that mockingbirds actually mimicked other birds slightly more than ten percent of the time.

Greater Sulphur-crested Cockatoo

Still, they do copy. But why? That isn't too clear either. There are other birds that mimic naturally: starlings, marsh warblers, robinchats, lyrebirds, drongos, and many more. Some of them imitate as a general rule, having virtually no song of their own remaining. It has been suggested that singing has become less of a territorial imperative for some species; the advertising function has diminished and song is no longer needed for its recognition value. For highly territorial mockingbirds, that is hardly the case. The reason for their mockery remains a puzzle.

A similar mystery of mimicry involves those birds that can be taught to talk by people, notably parrots; macaws; cockatoos; crows; ravens; other corvids; and the starling group, especially mynas. Technically they shouldn't be able to imitate people. Anatomically, they don't have the equipment; more studies are necessary to learn how they do it.

A more intriguing question is why? It would be logical to assume that

38

it serves a purpose in nature. Yet despite decades of investigation, there is no proof that they ever use this talent in the wild.

The evidence remains to be assembled, but there are theories. Some behavioral experts believe talking parallels the human baby's early attempts to speak. Few parrots (the family *Psittacidae*) become good talkers unless they are acquired as young birds. That fact dovetails nicely with the manner in which most are obtained for the pet trade: by robbing nest sites. The parrot is usually not long past the chick stage when it becomes somebody's pet.

As pets, parrots, mynas, and the like are kept in fairly close contact with people, but isolated from their own kind. They are naturally sociable birds, and their social inclinations are transferred to humans. As owner talks to pet, the bird responds with a vocalization, ultimately hitting an approximation of the owner's words. Such a response earns the master's approval. Plus greater attention, increased socializing. The talking birds, among the more intelligent species in the first place, learn to make more imitative sounds. The more they talk, the more attention they get. In relatively short order, the cage is occupied by a feathered talk-show host.

13 ❖ How do porcupines shoot their quills?

The North American porcupine (*Erethizon dorsatum*) is an arboreal critter—it spends a lot of time in trees. When it feels threatened, it makes a beeline for the nearest tree. Sometimes the animal is caught flat-footed, waddling out in the open, and the bristly rodent adopts one of the best defensive postures in the animal kingdom.

If you have ever encountered one of them on the ground, chances are you have had no more than a glimpse of anything other than "porky's" rear end. Because its most vulnerable features are the face and stomach, both quill-less, the animal's goal is to keep those parts turned away from the attacker at all times.

At the same time the porcupine counterattacks. It swats at the enemy with its cactuslike tail. The quills are barbed and wicked; they will catch at and stick to anything with which they come into contact. These sometimes lethal weapons are also loosely attached.

When the porcupine's tail is flailing about vigorously, the quills, loos-

Canadian Porcupine

ened even more by now, pull out easily if they strike something. Like the nose of a dog with more courage than sense. The quills attach and imbed themselves instantly. It almost seems as if they were flying into the opponent. As if the porcupine really had launched a barrage of painful needles. Nothing of the kind.

It all happens so rapidly and easily, it merely looks that way. Cross off another legend.

A dramatic variation of Porcupine Power is provided by the crested porcupines (the genus *Hystrix*) of Africa and Asia. They pack the same basic defensive armament as their American cousins, albeit their quills are barbless. Crested porcupines are ground dwellers, and, at the first hint of trouble, they make a dash for their burrows. Unless that escape route is cut off. In that case, the porcupine shifts into reverse and runs backward toward its enemy. It has been written: The best defense is a good offense.

14 ❖ *Do animals play?*

Yes, and often it is nothing more than fun and games. A monkey waving and tossing a stick, for example. Polar bears (*Thalarctos maritimus*) have been known to while away hours in amusement with stones, even balancing these crude toys on their heads.

Most animal playtime is serious business: a pleasurable way to develop survival skills. Next time you're at a zoo, watch lion cubs playing. One will crouch low against the ground, stalk slowly toward its littermate, and pounce on the surprised "victim." It's the beginning of a knockabout wrestling match, with the cubs cuffing each other harmlessly. Wolves, tigers, cheetahs, raccoons, coyotes—carnivores in general—engage in such roughhouse sessions. It's cute, delightful to watch —and some of the most serious combat of their lives. They are learning, practicing, developing the abilities that will make them efficient predators.

Among monkeys and apes, playing lays the foundation for social

Lowland Gorilla

order—a requirement for the survival of primate communities. Through play-fighting, a young monkey learns—in a way that minimizes the possibility of both physical and psychological injury—where it stands in relation to its peers. Individuals victorious in the "matches" of infancy are most likely to play a dominant role when they reach maturity. Others lower on the ladder have, by then, accepted this as normal. Since they know their places, the possibility of serious, potentially fatal, clashes between adults reduces sharply.

In the simian kindergarten, infants also catch on quickly that it is courting disaster to tangle with their older brothers, sisters, and cousins. The previous generation is bigger, stronger, faster, and more adept in monkey martial arts. Still, conflicts do occur. There are those who will, as young adults, challenge their elders for position, possibly even the top spot. They acquire the combat seasoning and skills necessary for advancement during the scuffles of youth. This type of behavior is not restricted to primates. Elephants, for example, also depend on playing to establish social order.

Many hoofed mammals also engage in play. In herds of Mongolian wild horses (*Equus przewalskii*), the breeding stallion will play-fight with his offspring. Father is helping the colts to develop dexterity and physical coordination that will help them to hold their own against predators. Or better yet, to avoid predators.

It appears that even whales play—at least some of the order *Cetacea* do. A bumptious calf will perform all sorts of acrobatic gyrations on and around its mother—sliding over her tail, wiggling across her back, standing on its head or rolling in the water, slapping its own tail or flipper against the water's surface. Infants can even fire themselves upward, almost completely out of the water—an act called breaching. Because whales are so difficult to study, it is not yet possible to state with certainty what, if any, purpose these antics serve. Possibly they help to cement the bond between mother and offspring.

The examples could continue and they would continue to be about mammals. Some ornithologists are convinced that a few of the brainier birds, such as crows and ravens, play. Maybe so, but the subject demands more inquiry. At this point on the research clock, mammals dominate the playground.

15 ❖ *What is behind a monkey's smile?*

Fear. A monkey smiles in submission to a dominant member of its troop. The grin—a slightly pained one, to be sure—denotes that the

Diana Monkey

animal knows its place and will not dispute a superior. Not to smile might invite an attack. Hence, fear, not pleasure, triggers the grin. Which is why behaviorists are more likely to call it a grimace.

It's all part of the extensive communication repertoire evolved by monkeys and other primates to keep their sophisticated social systems functioning. While most of the facial expressions, vocalizations, gestures, and body postures that make up monkey linguistics may confuse the average human observer, it is probably monkeys' mobile faces that lead to the most misinterpretation. The look, as people interpret it, may even mean something quite contradictory to what the monkey understands; a kiss is not just a kiss, a sigh is not just a sigh.

Apropos of the latter, a yawn may be a threat. There is no greater way to display teeth—especially if done in profile—as a reminder of the weaponry at a monkey's disposal should another animal challenge it. This meaning is never more evident than in the yawn of a large male baboon, displaying a set of canines that can tear open flesh as easily as a chain saw. In different circumstances, a monkey's yawn can be an expression of frustration. At times, this overdeveloped sighing is actually the result of fatigue.

As for the rest of the lyric, monkeys are often affectionate but they don't exactly kiss. They will pucker their lips, moving them in and out rapidly in what people might recognize as a "kissy-kiss" invitation. It is a supplication all right: a submissive request to be groomed.

One of the more notable cases of human misinterpretation of a nonhuman primate's face occurred with an ape. Early in the American space program, a chimpanzee named Ham was sent up and rocketed into orbit around the Earth, the first anthropoid to achieve such distinction. When he landed and was removed from the capsule, someone exclaimed, "He must have enjoyed the trip. Look, he's smiling!" No way. Ham was scared right out of his orbit.

16 ❖ Why does a rattlesnake shake its rattle?

To warn you or any other careless animal: Don't step on it, don't crowd its space. Menacing as the rattlesnake (genus *Crotalus*) may seem to you, it feels threatened. If something about the adversary's behavior suggests to the snake that the deterrent is not working, it will not hesitate to bring out the heavy artillery. Yet, given the option, the rattler would rather twitch than fight; it just wants to be left alone.

Many herpetologists believe that the roots of rattling lie back in the

Pleistocene era when these serpents were evolving on the prairies. At that time the grasslands were heavily populated by hoofed animals. The chances of getting stepped on by something heavy and sharp were immense. So the snakes got their own defensive warning system.

Unfortunately, the snake does not always have the opportunity to send signals. If, without looking, you step over a log and plant your boot squarely on a rattlesnake, it won't waste time on niceties. Even if you merely startle the snake by passing, the chances of a strike are high. Often, when the weather is cold—in early spring or autumn—rattlers tend to be lethargic and may not set off an alarm. They may not even strike if it's cold enough.

The rest of the good news is that not many people are bitten by rattlesnakes and very few die from such wounds. In the United States, fewer than half-a-dozen fatalities a year. If you are prone to worry about that sort of thing, you would do better to shift your concern to being struck by thunderbolts, a much more likely possibility.

You may imagine that the sound issuing from a vibrating rattle will resemble the maracas in a Latin dance band. Not so. If you are in the vicinity of a rattler sending signals and you pause to listen at a safe distance, you will hear a sort of electrified buzz. Adding to the mechanized image, the buzz winds up or down in intensity as the snake becomes more or less agitated. On the other hand, some Indian tribes have appropriated snake rattles as the key ingredient in their ritualistic noisemakers. Those instruments do sound more like what we think of as rattles; that's because people can't shake like snakes.

A newborn rattlesnake has only a hard button at the end of its tail—not much of a warning device. As the reptile grows, a segment is added each time it sheds its skin. That can happen several times a year when the animal is young. Ultimately eight segments per rattle is about average, regardless of age. The tip breaks off occasionally as more and more segments are added.

There is even a rattleless rattlesnake (*Crotalus catalinensis*), which is found only on Santa Catalina Island in the Gulf of California, off Mexico's Baja peninsula. In every other respect it is unquestionably a rattlesnake. It behaves like one, too. Though its rattle is nothing more than a silent, vestigial button, the snake vibrates its tail against the earth to produce noise.

There are several other species of snake that shake their tails, drumming them against dry leaves for a buzzing effect. Black racers (*Coluber constrictor*) do it all the time. Presumably this is also intended as a warning; whether or not this behavior evolved as a means of frightening potential attackers by imitating the rattlesnake is difficult to say, but it is a reasonable possibility.

17 ❖ *Why do woodchucks hibernate in winter?*

Why not? There's nothing to eat, and eating is the favorite pastime of the woodchuck (*Marmota monax*). Cold weather virtually eliminates the staples of its diet: various grasses and leafy plants, especially the kinds you have planted in your backyard. Around the end of summer, the woodchuck's internal clock, probably activated by the number of daylight hours, signals that it's time to stoke up. The animal pursues its vocation, stripping fields and gardens with a dedication to gluttony that is awesome. Ask any farmer.

Barely pausing for breath, the woodchuck stores up fat. It is not unusual for one to weigh as much as fourteen pounds. Its food supply now self-contained, the roly-poly rodent burrows underground to await the return of spring.

Having tucked in, the animal goes into a sort of suspended animation. If you found one, you would swear it was dead. Its metabolism slows down greatly; the heartbeat is almost undetectable. Body temperature lowers and blood flows at a much slower rate so that the woodchuck consumes food—its fat—very slowly.

The animal remains in this snug state until March or April. It is highly unlikely that a woodchuck, or "groundhog," will awaken on February 2nd. Not in Punxatawny, Pennsylvania, or anywhere else. If it did it would not look for its shadow. It would seek another woodchuck. Object: mating. For that is the woodchuck's second favorite pastime.

In the Snow Belt, quite a few nonmigrating animals hibernate, mostly for the same reason: no food. Ground squirrels (genus *Callospermophilus*) do it. Insect-eating bats have no prey available so they retire to caves and spend the winter hanging upside down. Chipmunks (the genus *Eutamias*) effect a sort of compromise. Prior to going underground they store seeds, nuts, and grains in chambers within their burrows. They do go into a deep winter sleep—not as comalike as the woodchuck's—but they wake up occasionally to have a meal, then doze off again.

Reptiles also hibernate, but inadequate food is only part of the reason. The turtle walled up in mud on the river bottom and the rattlesnake coiled with companions in a den are there because these creatures lack the ability of mammals to regulate their own body temperatures internally. Usually—and incorrectly—called "cold-blooded" (theirs is as warm as anybody else's), reptiles depend on an external source, sunlight, for thermal adjustments to keep them functioning. That's why they spend so much time sunning themselves.

Woodchuck

One more thing, and let's be perfectly clear about this: Bears (of the family *Ursidae*) *do not* hibernate. Like the woodchucks, they have gorged themselves during summer and have stored fat. But they merely sleep; there is no slowdown of the bears' metabolic rate comparable to the woodchuck's, and their body temperature does not lower. They are able to make use of the fat supply when food is scarce, but they are likely to wake up at any time and search outside for food. It is best to respect the "do not disturb" sign on a bear den.

Birds, of course, solve the winter food problem by migrating and have no need to hibernate. Or do they? Long ago, Indians in the North American west told of a bird spending entire winters holed up, never venturing forth from recesses along the walls of canyons. Ornithologists dismissed tales suggesting a hibernating bird as legend, pure and simple. Until the early 1950s.

At which point somebody apparently scaled a canyon wall and discovered a hibernating bird. It is a member of the nightjar family, the poor-will (*Phalaenoptilus nuttallii*). It is not yet known whether every individual member of the species hibernates, but some definitely do.

Insects are the dietary staple of the poor-will. When warm weather disappears, so does the food supply. So the birds climb into crevices and sink into a season-long sleep. While they are sleeping, they almost cease to breathe. Digestive functions stop. Their normal body temperature of 102°F falls to about 65°F. Researchers have also learned, by banding birds, that some poor-wills return to the same hibernation hole winter after winter.

18 ❖ *Why do fireflies flash?*

Usually they're turned on by sex. That may seem flippant, but it's fairly accurate. Most of the time, these beetles—not flies at all—of the family *Lampyridae* are seeking mates when they light up. The luminescence of the firefly is cold light, chemically induced by the interaction of the compound luciferin with oxygen and the enzyme luciferase inside the insect's abdomen. Once triggered, the lovelight glows through the fire-fly's translucent skin.

Another major reason for flashing is that the insect is alarmed—disturbed by another animal, a possible predator, or even young boys who like to make living lanterns by stuffing fireflies into glass jars.

Sexual signaling is done in code: The blinks must follow regularly patterned intervals if the message is to be received. The male flies about, illuminating himself. The female responds by flashing her own light. If she does so at intervals that the male recognizes as one of his own kind, he heads for her like an airplane pilot toward a beacon. If not, he keeps on flying.

Survival often depends on the ability to adapt, and the coding system of fireflies has produced a behavioral adaptation that is intriguing if not exactly cricket. Researcher James Lloyd discovered that in the American firefly genus *Photuris*, some females broke the code, so to speak, of the genus *Photinus*. This alien female is able to respond at proper intervals, luring a *Photinus* male to her. But when he arrives, eager to mate, he is in for a dreadful shock: The *Photuris* female, larger than he, grabs him and eats him. Humans should exercise extreme caution before attempting to draw moral lessons from this or any other form of animal behavior.

Katydids sing and crickets chirp for the same reason that fireflies flash: to locate a mate. Both make their music by rubbing wings together, albeit different wings—but that's another story. Katydids (the family *Tettigoniidae*) use the firefly method: Males and females send and receive signals, moving closer until they locate one another. Among crickets (the family *Gryllidae*) only the male chirps; he stays put while the female gradually homes in on the signal and finds her mate.

All these insects—indeed, most insects—signal after dark only. Signaling evolved as a nocturnal ritual because fewer insect-eating birds are on the wing at that hour. Daylight communicators are limited chiefly to the likes of grasshoppers and cicadas—snappy fliers with good eyesight.

50

19 ❖ Do all birds sit on eggs to incubate them?

Thousands—in fact, most—do, but there are some noteworthy exceptions. Chief among them are the megapodes (the scientific way of saying "big feet") of Australia, New Guinea, and various islands nearby. Also known as incubator birds, mound-builders, or thermometer birds, the ten species depend on sun or soil or vegetation or variable mixtures of all three, rather than body heat, to incubate their eggs, the only birds to do so.

The most ambitious, the scrub fowl, (*Megapodius freycinet*) scratches together leaves, grasses, sundry plants, and sandy soil and erects a mound that may reach fifteen feet in height and thirty-five feet in diameter. (The bird itself is only about twenty inches long.) Not only do males and females cooperate on construction, but several pairs merge to engineer a community incubator. Since this is a formidable project, the mound is used for many seasons. Tunnels as long as three feet are burrowed into it and the eggs laid within. The decomposing vegetation—in effect, a sort of maternal mulch—plus the sun warm the eggs to the point of hatching.

Brush turkeys (*Alectura lathami*) build similar but smaller pyramids that are almost exclusively vegetable matter. The fermenting plants generate so much heat on the steamy jungle hillsides where brush turkeys live that overheating is a danger. The male probes the pile with his beak and tongue to test the temperature, then digs into and rearranges vegetation to adjust it. Not until he is satisfied that conditions are correct does he permit the female to lay her eggs inside. He continues to monitor and adjust temperature throughout the incubation period.

Brush Turkey

There is precious little vegetation in the Australian scrubland habitat of the mallee fowl, or ocellated megapode (*Lipoa ocellata*). The male digs a pit in the sand, scrapes together what leaf litter and other plants he can muster, and covers that with a layer of sandy soil. Temperatures can fluctuate wildly in this environment, so the male is kept extremely busy checking and adjusting heat levels, scraping away layers of soil, rotating it, sometimes even tearing the upper level apart and rebuilding. Because the female lays her eggs at irregular intervals, the male spends eleven months of the year on incubation duty. By contrast, the maleo (*Megacephalon*) excavates a pit on the beach, deposits eggs, throws on a cover of sand, and departs for good. Some maleos place the egg pits in the vicinity of volcanoes so that subterranean steam handles the warming chores.

Then there are birds that don't bother to build anything, much less sit on it, even though their eggs depend on body heat for incubation. These are brood parasites, those that lay their eggs in other birds' nests, thrusting foster parenthood on unsuspecting neighbors who get stuck with all the work. Parasitic representatives appear in some six families of birds, but the most notorious are the cuckoos (the family *Cuculidae*). Not all cuckoos are practicing parasites, but some are so clever they have evolved the ability to lay eggs that imitate the appearance of the eggs of whatever bird species is unwittingly playing host. Once the intruding eggs are incubated and hatched by the surrogate parents, the baby cuckoos put their own adaptive strategies to work. The hatchling may well kick its roommates, who belong there, out of the nest and grab all the food for itself.

Birds of the polar regions lack standard nesting materials and adopt alternatives to nest-sitting. The emperor penguin (*Aptenodytes fosteri*) flouts conventional human wisdom by mating on the Antarctic ice shelf during winter. Having laid her egg, the female transfers it to her mate, then toddles some fifty or sixty miles across the ice to the sea and dives in to feed for the first time in weeks. The male takes over the egg with his own built-in incubator. Holding the egg on top of his feet, he folds a pouch of skin from his lower abdomen over it, covering it securely. Once on incubator duty, he dare not expose the precious egg to ice or the frigid air. The emperor, who is living off stored fat, must maintain this stance until the egg hatches, more than sixty days later. He does this in the face of almost nonstop gale-force winds, temperatures of minus-forty degrees Fahrenheit, and a wind/chill factor too depressing even to calculate. The female returns just in time with stomach stuffed so she can regurgitate food for the hatchling. Not for a few years do penguin chicks realize—if, indeed, they ever do—what they owe their parents.

20 ❖ Why do lions live in prides?

Lion society was unraveled by Dr. George Schaller, Director of the New York Zoological Society's Animal Research and Conservation Center, who spent three years in Tanzania's Serengeti National Park observing predator/prey relationships. The "King of Beasts" is the only feline that has embraced communal living—though packs are common in dogdom—and the reasons lie in diet and landscape.

Adult lions (*Panthera leo*) average about 400 pounds, some hitting 500. A healthy male can wolf down seventy-five pounds of meat during one meal. Their natural prey tends to be correspondingly big and beefy: wildebeest, oryx, eland, sable, and other large antelope, zebras, warthogs, sometimes buffalo. As many a rodeo cowboy has learned, it is no cinch to pull down a moving target that weighs several hundred pounds all by yourself.

Successful ambushing of king-sized prey requires a team effort. As when one lion pursues a single antelope, driving it toward a waiting partner. Or when several lions encircle, then charge, small herds. Hunting parties may be composed of duos, perhaps half a dozen or more. Dr. Schaller's notes showed that two lions literally scored twice as well against big game as solo performers.

Cheetahs, leopards, and smaller cats make their livings from prey more consistent with their own size: impala, gazelles, baboons, monkeys, jackals, various birds. Barring rare strokes of good fortune, it is well nigh impossible for a leopard or cheetah to drop the likes of a zebra. And when the catch is small, there is nothing to share. Which makes for an asocial lifestyle.

Other felines are also equipped to adopt different hunting strategies.

Leopards (*Panthera pardus*) are sneaks. Their usual hunting grounds are along forest and river edges, amid boulders, anywhere that stealth and surprise can be put to advantage. Cheetahs (*Acinonyx jubatus*) operate out in the open, but they rely on their remarkable speed. Lions are too large and, relatively speaking, too slow for such tactics.

African Lions

Tigers (*Panthera tigris*) are not exactly midgets either; some exceed lion-size. Yet they hunt alone. They also do it in dense, often dark forests where abundant vegetation supplies camouflaging shadows and ample cover. Prey animals in Asian forests are generally more widely dispersed than their counterparts on the African plains. The tiger stands a better chance going one-on-one.

Out in the wide open spaces of the savanna, with little or nothing to hide behind, lions are eminently visible; partnership becomes essential. Especially for males. With their massive bulk and their can't-do-a-thing-with-it hairstyles, they are about as inconspicuous as an eighteen-wheeler cruising an Interstate across a Kansas prairie. It is for that reason that females handle most of the hunting, not because males are lazy, lumpish, chauvinistic louts.

Mind you, lions do pursue smaller game, such as gazelles, success-fully, and individuals can work by themselves. Exceptions notwithstand-ing, life to a lion means a diet of large prey animals whose habitat is open landscape. The best way to cope with those requirements is to pool resources. Thus, the pride.

Dr. Schaller also uncovered several subsidiary benefits to group liv-ing. If males fail to star as hunters, they serve the pride in other capaci-ties. Bringing up the rear, they protect the cubs who can't keep up and are vulnerable to other predators. Lions' sense of community does not necessarily extend to sharing the wealth: Mothers often let cubs go hungry while gorging themselves at a kill. Yet males sometimes share with youngsters.

At an earlier stage of life, a cub may be famished for milk only to find its mother less than enthusiastic about nursing. The hungry tot will implore female after female until, usually, it finds one willing to stand in as foster mother and suckle it. Indeed the pride functions as a kind of day-care center, helping to train cubs for their future roles in coopera-tive hunting.

Not only cubs benefit. If a kill is large enough, there may be food for sick or injured members. A lion under the weather has more going for it than an unhealthy leopard. Out on the savanna, one dare not leave one's meal untended or other predators and scavengers will swarm in like uninvited neighbors at a backyard barbecue. The pride's labor surplus allows some members to stand guard while others refresh themselves with a drink or a snooze. The lion may or may not be king of beasts, but it is surely one of the most organized.

21 ❖ Why do woodpeckers peck?

Most birds "fence-in" territories with melody. Woodpeckers (the family *Picidae*), as the rhythm section of the bird world, drum on hollow trees to advertise their home grounds and issue invitations to prospective mates to join them there. The male's impulse to batter trees may be triggered by the drumming of a neighboring male, proclaiming *his* territory. The birds specifically seek out hollow objects—tree trunks, branches, stumps—in order to augment the volume. In urban areas they frequently use television aerials and drain pipes for the same purpose.

Woodpeckers peck for other reasons but the quality of sound differs; none make as much racket as the mating solicitation. A "pecker" will hammer incessantly at a tree, a telephone pole, even wooden pilings on piers, and bore right in to create a nest hole. Some species make burrows in the ground. If he's going to lure a female to follow him home, the male had better have a place ready where they can raise a family. When the mating fever has cooled, either a male or female is likely to drill a hole for no other reason than to find lodgings and get a good night's sleep.

The birds can bore into wood with relative ease because woodpecker bills are as straight and as hard as chisels. Once the woodpeckers abandon a hole, other birds with less substantial equipment often take up residence.

Drumming is also evidence of a search for food. The woodpecker drills into tree bark, then probes inside with its incredibly long and flexible tongue in order to dine on ants, grubs, beetles, even the sap of trees.

Percussion aside, woodpeckers do have calls. None of the approximately 200 species is reputed to be melodious, but they are loud.

What with chiseling away on a hard object with a force and speed reminiscent of a jackhammer, the woodpecker would seem a likely candidate for concussions. Its long tongue prevents such casualties. That organ rolls back and coils up into the rear of the skull, forming a cushion. For all that is known, woodpeckers don't even get headaches.

22 ❖ Antlers and horns look like wicked weapons, yet deer and antelope rarely injure each other during territorial battles. Why?

Apparently they follow rules. Most duels of this sort center around the antlers of male deer (or horns, if it's male antelope you're concerned with), and though the competition is intense, it contains a strong element of ritual. The opponents square off with a great deal of posturing and jockeying for advantage. Literally locking antlers, they push each other back and forth for what frequently seems an interminable length of time. Ultimately one realizes that victory will not be his. The loser breaks away and runs. Winners are nearly always the biggest and strongest animals in the neighborhood and they carry the most imposing sets of antlers.

Serious injuries rarely occur during these contests. Wounds, even nicks, are not that common. Death is usually a fluke. Yet the same imposing antlers and horns, used differently, can become lethal weapons against would-be predators. The battling animals aren't trying to kill each other, thanks to the code of the wild. If dominant males wiped out all of their challengers—or vice-versa—they would be hurrying their species toward extinction. Hence they fight cleanly even though the stakes are the highest possible: dominance and the right to mate with all the females.

Wild cattle—the American buffalo, to name one species—follow the same combative course. With our native bison (*Bison bison*), it's strictly a pushing-shoving contest. Bighorn sheep (*Ovis canadensis*) stage the most spectacular jousts in the animal kingdom. Squaring off at some distance, two rams lower their heads and race full speed at each other until they bash horns and bounce apart. As the explosive din of contact echoes across the valleys, the combatants return to their respective corners. They repeat the sequence again and again—sometimes for several hours—until one admits defeat and departs, perhaps to seek a wild equivalent of aspirin.

Pere David Deer

23 ❖ *Why do vampire bats suck blood?*

The tiny flying mammals' bizarre—to us—feeding behavior and dietary preference, as well as our general queasiness about bats, have spawned a host of legends and thousands of feet of spine-chilling motion picture film. The image of the vampire bat (*Desmodus rotundus*) definitely needs work.

For openers, the bat, which ranges across much of Central and South America, is utterly unfaithful to its Transylvanian namesakes. It does not *suck* blood. The vampire *laps* up the liquid, like a kitten at a saucer of milk.

Alighting softly on its victim, the bat uses its surgically sharp incisors to make a shallow cut in the skin. Blood flows from the wound, and the bat licks the fluid. A chemical in the bat's saliva prevents coagulation, so blood flows continually until the bat is bloated and ready for take-off. Which does not mean several quarts later. How much blood could a bat that measures three inches from head to tail manage to drain away? Perhaps an ounce a day.

Consider: Even if sixteen vampires decide to take their meal at your bloodstream, the most you will lose is the pint you intended to donate to the Red Cross. And, if you fail to notice sixteen bats—even tiny ones—landing on your person, you are probably not long for this world anyway.

Why the plasma diet? Because that is the only thing this animal can digest. In some very distant past other food, or competition for it, was too dear, apparently, so the family *Desmodontidae* found this substitute source of nourishment. Vampire bat stomachs evolved as long skinny tubes like soda straws, much reduced from the convoluted plumbing of

Vampire Bats

other mammals, including other bats. This simple stomach suited the liquid diet, and the vampires developed a highly specialized behavior pattern to go with their physiological limitations.

Vampire bats are rather indiscriminate about where they sip their supper. Originally they dined on deer, peccaries, large birds. The growth of agriculture in Latin America has meant greater opportunity to put the bite on domestic cattle, swine, sheep, goats, poultry, and so on. And there has been a corresponding boom in the vampire population.

Nor are the bats above a little human blood, although it is difficult to come up with verified cases of punctures in the neck. A foot protruding from beneath a blanket would be a more likely target. Not only do they land like feathers, but your experienced vampires make the incision so neatly you'll never notice. When your younger vamps dig in, they tend to bruise the flesh in a way that is instantly noticeable.

Not to worry. There is no evidence that anyone has ever perished from the bite of a *healthy* vampire. Healthy is the key word. Some vampire bats do carry rabies. That is their real danger to people and livestock. Yet rabid bats represent a small percentage of the total population, so it is not recommended that you stock up on crucifixes, wolfbane, mystic incantations, or Eucharistic bread before a trip to Mexico. A necklace of garlic will only make you smell like a salami factory. It might even attract vampire bats.

24 ❖ *Why do many animals stop and spray here, there, everywhere?*

Nothing random about it, despite appearances. They are using their urine to scent-mark, not relieving themselves, and it's an essential survival technique.

Wolves, tigers, lions, leopards, and other predators occupy very large territories, sometimes more than a hundred square miles. Clearly the "owners" cannot be everywhere at once. Boundaries must be sharply defined. As the animal moves about in its other normal activities, it pauses frequently to sprinkle urine on trees, rocks, moss, logs, grass, anything handy. It is literally outlining its territory as surely as if it were to erect a wire fence around the perimeter. To keep barriers up, warn invaders away, and forestall territorial skirmishes, the animal scent-marks at pretty much every opportunity. Your domestic dog or cat still has the habit if not the need. Its territory is defined more by you than any call of the wild.

The Indian rhinoceros (*Rhinoceros unicornis*) does virtually the same thing, dragging its feet through its own piles of dung. During the rhino's travels, small amounts of dung drop from its feet. The big beast

Ring-tailed Lemur

thereby draws an imaginary line, extending its presence as if it had deposited a giant dung pile.

Ring-tailed lemurs (*Lemur catta*), primitive, foxy-faced primates, organize their social lives with glands that secrete odorous fluids. For example, these territorial animals keep busy doing handstands, lifting their posteriors to mark objects with glandular fragrances from below their tails.

25 ❖ Monkeys seem to spend a lot of time picking bugs off each other. Why?

Grooming does absorb a lot of monkey hours, but personal hygiene is more of a secondary result. The chief benefits to the monkeys are social and psychological.

Talapoin Monkey

It is vital to their survival that each troop of monkeys functions as a cohesive social unit. Grooming reinforces group bonds, the links between individuals. It appears to be as important to the groomer as to the groomee. When you see a mob of monkeys grooming each other, you may reasonably assume they are quite content.

The animals higher up on the dominance ladder, especially the Big Chief, are most often the recipients of such favors. Yet they, too, will groom others in the band. It's a calming, tension-relieving occupation for them and provides reassurance for both parties.

On the hygiene front, it does help to maintain a healthy monkey. When they probe and pick and fuss through one another's fur, they remove particles of dirt, flecks of dry skin, and annoying ticks.

Most nonhuman primates do it: apes, baboons, lemurs, even those, like marmosets, that live in small family groups rather than large troops. There is no telling how far mankind would have progressed had we not discarded social grooming somewhere down the evolutionary pike.

❖ *Epilogue*

Behaviorism: What's in it for you? The behaviorist has become an important citizen in today's world and the role demands considerable dedication. If you are intrigued enough to pursue this interest on a professional level, that desire mandates a lengthy educational process. It so happens that many of the landmark behavioral studies were written as dissertations for doctoral degrees.

Should you be reluctant to embark on such a program, the study of animal behavior need not be denied you. After all, there were no graduate courses in ethology when Charles Darwin made his discoveries. Darwin also just happened to be a genius. And by today's standards he was an amateur, albeit a gifted amateur. Mostly he was a keen observer. With a little time and patience, observing is something you can do with the best of them.

Depending on how you are situated, backyards and nearby wooded areas or meadows make fine study sites. Such luminaries as Von Frisch and Lorenz learned plenty in such locations. Before you go, check field guides and other reference books for seasonal changes to give yourself a better shot at watching courtship, mating, and rearing of young. Regular observations are more likely to produce results. Binoculars help a lot. Above all, be quiet, don't move around. Try to identify individual animals. Look for resident populations. Be alert to repeated behavioral patterns. And sounds.

Many nature centers as well as state and national parks have blinds in which you can watch animals at close range without disturbing them. If you have the appropriate spot available on your own property —near a pond favored by waterfowl, for instance—build your own blind or "hide." It might be a tent with peepholes or a three-sided wooden shack with holes or slits through which you can watch comfortably. The important thing is to prevent the animals from seeing you. (It also helps to have a roof in case the weather changes abruptly.) If you want to formalize your study a little more, join a local nature club or birdwatching group.

One of the best places to observe natural animal behavior is a zoo or aquarium. Particularly if your interests lean toward exotic wildlife. You might assume that the artificial environment of a zoo is too unnatural, but, in modern zoos, the animals act quite normally. If you require proof, look no further than the photographs in this book. Nearly all were taken not far from my office at the Bronx Zoo in New York City.

As a matter of fact, zoos have proven a boon to professional behaviorists. Especially in cases where animals are exceedingly difficult to encounter, much less observe, under totally natural conditions. Often behavior noted in a zoological park or aquarium provides clues that help a researcher know what to look for in the wild. Sometimes zoo behavior is confirmed later by sightings in the wild. Not long ago we published an article in our magazine *Animal Kingdom*, in which a Houston Zoo curator described the hatching and rearing of a rare and exquisite South American bird, the cock-of-the-rock. A few months later we heard from a field researcher who witnessed much the same thing in the Peruvian rain forest. Confirmation for both parties.

The zoo/aquarium suggestion assumes that your local zoological park, or its aquatic counterpart, is a progressive facility with good natural habitat exhibits that more or less duplicate actual settings. A proper up-to-date zoo will also display social species in reasonably large groups—herds, packs, prides—so they can establish the same sort of relationships that would exist in the wild.

The naturalistic displays do encourage natural behavior. If you walk through the famous World of Birds at the Bronx Zoo you'll see, among other things, birds engaging in normal courtship and nesting activities. Even if you traveled thousands of miles on safari you would probably not get such a clear, close-up view. Or if you were to ride the monorail through our Wild Asia section you might see tiger cubs romping and frisking in the woods, playfully stalking one another only a few feet away from the train—just as they would in the Asian forest. Or visit the San Diego Wild Animal Park where the train will carry you past enormous exhibits, replicas of various geographic locales, in which many different species interact.

Some of the more imaginative American zoos are experimenting with what is called behavioral engineering. Just outside Chicago, the Brookfield Zoo offers several such exhibits. In the Small Cat Ecology House there is a remarkably realistic night-time North African desert scene in which sand cats probe behind rocks in order to forage for food. The cat's paw, unseen by the public, triggers a lever that releases a tidbit that drops at another spot, sending the cat scurrying after it. Just down the hall in this building, fishing cats do indeed catch real live fish from a jungle pool.

At the zoo in Tulsa, Oklahoma, there is an artificial termite mound on Chimp Island. The chimpanzees break off stems of grass, probe a hole in the mound for "termites" (though it's really mustard and the apes dote on it), and lick this treat from the grass. Visitors are thus able to watch bonafide tool-using behavior, just as Jane Goodall described it. Such mechanical contrivances serve a dual purpose: They reveal for visitors some aspects of animal behavior they would be unlikely to see otherwise, and they make life a lot more interesting for captive animals.

Herewith a few hints about *your* behavior if you aim to do behavioral research at the zoo:

1. Go early. Almost all the animals are more active before midday. They also become active late in the day but, by then, the zoo is much more crowded with people.

2. Go often. You won't be able to chart behavioral patterns if you make random visits.

3. Take your time. You'll spot a lot more going on if you remain near an exhibit for an hour or so. Prolonged viewing will open your head to greater understanding. Don't despair over the days when nothing much seems to happen.

4. Don't expect non-stop action. Or much action at all some days. Remember, sleeping is behaving, too, and some animals do a lot of that. You'll probably find activity levels higher among such creatures as monkeys and birds but they, too, stop and doze off occasionally.

5. Try to focus your attention on one species of animal. At least for a while. You'll learn more—and enjoy more—than if you adopt a shotgun approach.

6. Social groups are probably the most fun to watch. More interaction. Try to pick out individuals and track their behavior.

7. Mind your manners. Don't yell at the animals to provoke a reaction. And though it would seem unnecessary to say this, I'll say it anyway: Don't throw things to make the animals move. Don't feed them either. It's not only bad for them but it destroys their natural behavior.

8. If you can manage the dues, join the local zoological society. For one thing, you'll enjoy unlimited free admission to the zoo so you can observe as often as you wish. Many of these societies also sponsor lectures, film programs, and behind-the-scenes tours that can further your education.

9. Check out volunteer organizations. Many zoos and aquariums have such outfits attached to them. Usually they are called friends of the zoo or docents (i.e. teachers) and they often are an extension of the

68

zoo's education department. Such activities usually are geared to adults (though a college degree is not necessary) and, depending on the program, to teen-agers. Your responsibilities might include leading tours of schoolchildren and various adult groups. As you teach them you will learn as well—first, by being more intimately involved with your local zoological institution. And, before you can lead tours, you'll probably have to take a training course given by zoo/aquarium curators and educators. It's a unique opportunity to learn more about wildlife in a classroom where the objects of study are alive and behaving.

No, you won't be allowed to play with the animals. But sometimes dedicated volunteers become involved in projects that aid the zoo's scientific staff. At the National Zoo in Washington, D.C., volunteers have often assisted in behavioral monitoring such as "preg watch." When a special female animal—special by virtue of being rare or an endangered species—is nearing the end of her term of pregnancy, the volunteers keep a twenty-four-hour watch, recording every action. When birth seems imminent, they are prepared to summon staff curators and veterinarians.

On a few—and I must emphasize *few*—occasions, zoo volunteers wind up becoming zoo employees. I ought to know. I began my involvement with the New York Zoological Society as a volunteer guide at the Bronx Zoo.

The questions and answers in this volume aim to inform you of some of the more fascinating discoveries made about the lifestyles of animals. Perhaps the book can also dispel a few of the fantasies about animals that people seem reluctant to give up. With luck, this book will stimulate your own behavior—to read more, to watch better, and to get involved. Which is the first step toward preserving our wild heritage for future generations. It's nice to know that out there in the African jungle, wild chimpanzees do manufacture and use tools, even if they don't ride motorcycles. Once we begin to appreciate the behavior of animals, who knows what might happen? We might even begin to understand ourselves a little better.

❖ Suggested Reading

If you are sufficiently intrigued by the behavior of wild animals, you will want to read some of the following works. Although this list is not definitive, it does attempt to cover a wide range of animal species and includes some of the classics of behavioral literature. The majority are what publishers call "popular" (that is, nontechnical) books that almost anyone can understand. A few are straightforward scientific studies, which, while they do not pretend to be literary in the usual sense, are easily grasped and enjoyed by general readers. I call them "readable scientific studies" because most scientific tomes are reports of data that make no pretense toward narrative style but do contain lots of statistics and technical jargon. (Good bedtime reading for professional biologists.) A couple of titles are listed even though they are kind of "heavy"—for the benefit of advanced, more ambitious students of the subject. I have added cautions where appropriate so that readers may behave according to their own instincts.

1. Adamson, Joy. *Born Free*. Random House, 1974.
2. ———. *Spotted Sphinx*. Harcourt Brace Jovanovich, 1969.
3. Allen, Durwood. *Wolves of Minong: Their Vital Role in a Wild Community*. Houghton Mifflin, 1979.
4. BenDavid-Val, Leah, et al. *Discover Wildlife in Your Backyard*. National Wildlife Federation, 1977.
5. Bertram, Brian. *Pride of Lions*. Charles Scribner's Sons, 1978.
6. Craighead, Frank C., Jr. *Track of the Grizzly*. Sierra Club Books, 1979.
7. Craighead, John and Craighead, Frank. *Hawks, Owls, and Wildlife*. Dover, 1979.
8. Crowcroft, Peter. *The Life of the Shrew*. Max Reinhardt, 1975.
9. Darwin, Charles. *Voyage of the Beagle*. Anchor (Natural History Press) reprint, 1972.
10. Douglas-Hamilton, Iain and Oria. *Among the Elephants*. The Viking Press, 1975.
11. Fox, Michael. *Between Animal and Man*. Coward, McCann and Geohegan, 1976.
12. Hahn, Emily. *Look Who's Talking! New Discoveries in Animal Communication*. Thomas Y. Crowell, 1978.
13. Hapney, Peter W. *Rodents: Their Lives and Habits*. Taplinger, 1975.
14. Hediger, Heini. *Psychology and Behavior of Animals in Zoos and Circuses*. Dover, 1979.
15. ———. *Wild Animals in Captivity*. Dover, 1950.
16. Kruuk, Hans. *Hyaena*. Oxford University Press paperback, 1975. (This is an abridged, popularized version of the original scientific study, which is also quite readable: *The Spotted Hyena: A Study of Predation and Social Behavior*. University of Chicago Press, 1972.)
17. Lorenz, Konrad. *King Solomon's Ring*. New American Library, 1952.
18. ———. *Man Meets Dog*. Penguin, 1965.
19. Marler, Peter, et al. *The Marvels of Animal Behavior*. National Geographic Society, 1972.

20. McClintock, Dorcas. *A Natural History of Giraffes.* Charles Scribner's Sons, 1973.
21. ———. *A Natural History of Raccoons.* Charles Scribner's Sons, 1981.
22. ———. *A Natural History of Zebras.* Charles Scribner's Sons, 1976.
23. McDougal, Charles. *The Face of the Tiger.* Rivington Books, 1977.
24. Mech, L. David. *The Wolf.* Natural History Press. (A readable scientific study.)
25. Moss, Cynthia. *Portraits in the Wild: Behavior Studies of East African Mammals.* Houghton Mifflin, 1975.
26. Pryor, Karen. *Lads Before the Wind: Adventures in Porpoise Training.* Harper and Row, 1975.
27. Schaller, George. *The Deer and the Tiger: A Study of Wildlife in India.* University of Chicago Press, 1967. (A readable scientific study.)
28. ———. *Golden Shadows, Flying Hooves.* Knopf, 1973. (This is a popularized version of the original scientific study, which is also quite readable: *The Serengeti Lion: A Study of Predator-Prey Relations.* University of Chicago Press, 1972.)
29. ———. *Mountain Monarchs: Wild Sheep and Goats of the Himalaya.* University of Chicago Press, 1977. (A readable scientific study.)
30. ———. *Year of the Gorilla.* University of Chicago Press, 1964.
31. Tinbergen, Niko. *Animal Behavior.* Life Nature Library, 1965.
32. ———. *The Herring Gull's World.* Torch paperback, 1971. (Scientific study for advanced readers only.)
33. Van Lawick, Hugo and Van Lawick-Goodall, Jane. *Innocent Killers: A Fascinating Journey Through the Worlds of the Hyena, the Jackal, and the Wild Dog.* Houghton Mifflin, 1971.
34. Van Lawick-Goodall, Jane. *In the Shadow of Man.* Houghton Mifflin, 1971.
35. Wilson, Edward O. *Insect Societies.* Harvard University Press, 1971. (Scientific study for advanced readers only.)
36. ———. *Sociobiology: The New Synthesis.* Harvard University Press, 1975. (A readable scientific study.)

❖ *Index of Animals*